Open Roads!
A Kid's Guide to Eidfjord, Norway

Photography by John D. Weigand
Poetry by Penelope Dyan

Bellissima Publishing, LLC
Jamul, California
www.bellissimapublishing.com

Copyright © 2018 by Penny D. Weigand & John D. Weigand

All rights reserved. No part of this book may be reproduced or transmitted in any form or by any means, electronic or mechanical, including photocopying, recording, or by any other means, or by any information or storage retrieval system, without permission from the publisher.

ISBN 978-1-61477-332-0
First Edition

"There are many open roads from which you can choose.
The road you travel and how you travel it is all up to you."

PENELOPE DYAN

Open Roads!
Bellissima Publishing, LLC

Introduction

Eidfjord is the administrative center of Eidfjord; and it's a municipality located in Hordaland county, Norway. The village of Eidfjord is located at on the shore of the EidFjord on the inner branch of the large Hardangerfjorden. If that sounds like a mouthful, that's probably because it is. So perhaps the best thing to do is to remember that the Vikings were here and that this is a great place to visit!

Written by the award winning author, attorney and former teacher, Penelope Dyan, with photographs by John D. Weigand, you can practice your reading skills using this 'learn to read' book filled with word repetition, word recognition and rhyme, as you see a bit of what our author and photographer saw when they visited Eidfjord, Norway. And the size of this book with its extra large print fits perfectly in a kid-sized backpack! And this book also comes with a message just to get you thinking!

When you are all finished reading and practicing your reading skills, you can watch the free music video that goes with this book that you can find on Bellissimavideo's YouTube channel; and you can see even more of this beautiful Norwegian village!

Open Roads!
Bellissima Publishing, LLC

Open Roads!
A Kid's Guide to Eidfjord, Norway

Photography by John D. Weigand
Poetry by Penelope Dyan

A place of beauty is a feast for the eyes!
And this is something we all need to realize.
See the world as you walk along, because all of the world sings a beautiful song.

The smallest car can take you
here and there.
It can take you nearly everywhere!
Just ask your mother or father,
or ask your best friend,
or ask her sister or or her brother.
You think this car looks like a toy,
a perfect size for a girl or boy.
But mom looks at it and says ,
"That car would never fit
upon your shelf.
And this is a real car
that you could not possibly
drive all by yourself!"

Then Mom says to Dad,
"Look dear, Telsa has electric cars;
and they have free stations right here!"
And then you all stop,
as in the sun's light you all squint;
and you three begin a discussion
about your carbon footprint.

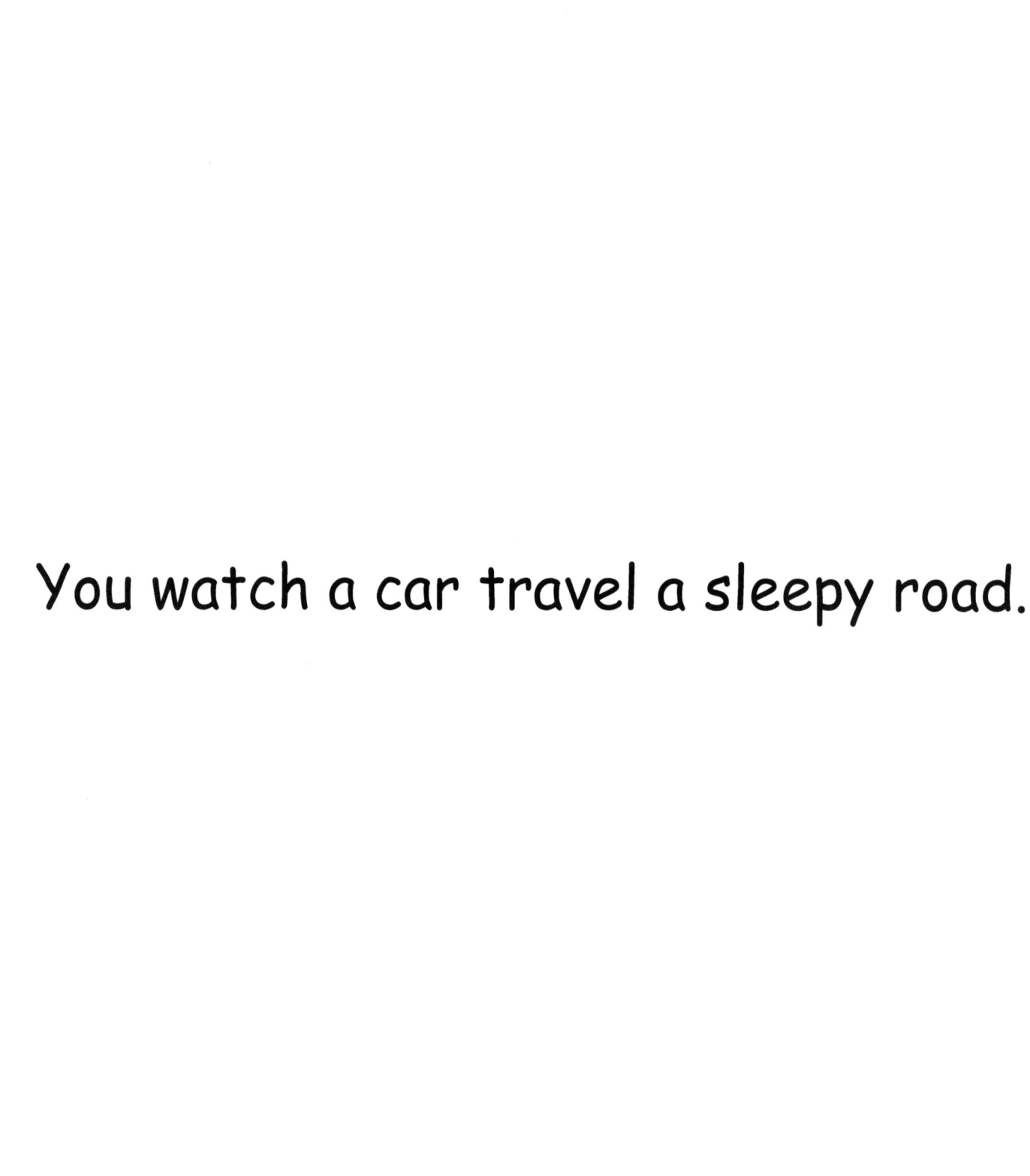

You watch a car travel a sleepy road.

You look down at the water blue.

You sit and you have a nice chat with a friendly moose, too!

And then you see the trolls!
They are having a party!
But there is something even more . . .

Mom buys you
a porcelain kitten in a teacup,
from a local souvenir store!

And then you all hop aboard
this bright blue and red train,
and you take in the sights
of the colorful Eidfjord terrain!

You see houses of red and white.

And then as another open road
you all travel down,
Mom says she's very impressed,
by this beautiful village town!
And your dad's mind seems to wander,
and the thought
of his own carbon imprint
he begins now to very carefully ponder.

And as your dad contemplates
his carbon footprint
in the sand,
he thinks about this small village
in this far off land.
And he decides that there must be
something that he can do,
to reduce his carbon footprint too!
And then you all decide
this is the lesson of the day,
as to your hotel you make your way!
And that night, as you lay in your bed,
visions of electric cars everywhere
fill up your head!

"This world is yours to have and to keep!"

PENELOPE DYAN

www.ingramcontent.com/pod-product-compliance
Ingram Content Group UK Ltd.
Pitfield, Milton Keynes, MK11 3LW, UK
UKHW060134240426
12048UKWH00002B/34